KU-299-936

...new coinage after his release from captivity in England in 1357. It included the first Scottish gold coin, the noble, worth six shillings and eight pence Scots. On the reverse, a king holds a sword and shield, standing on a ship ornamented with five lions. Only four of these coins are known still to exist.

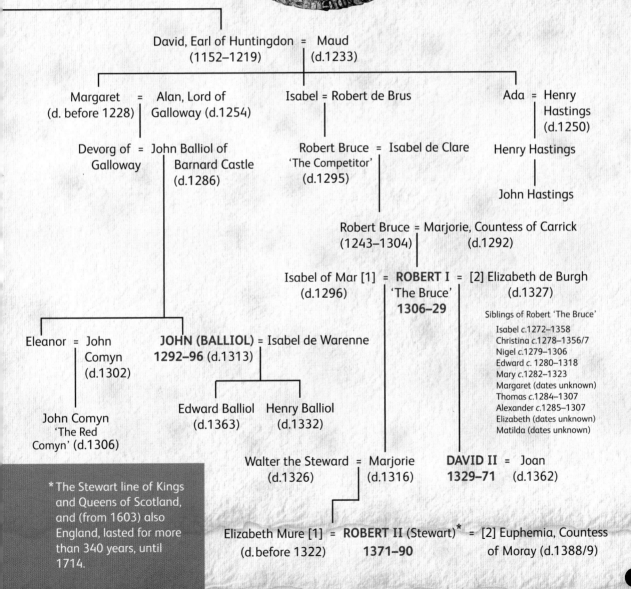

David, Earl of Huntingdon = Maud
(1152–1219) (d.1233)

Margaret = Alan, Lord of
(d. before 1228) Galloway (d.1254)

Isabel = Robert de Brus

Ada = Henry
Hastings
(d.1250)

Devorg of = John Balliol of
Galloway Barnard Castle
(d.1286)

Robert Bruce = Isabel de Clare
'The Competitor'
(d.1295)

Henry Hastings

John Hastings

Robert Bruce = Marjorie, Countess of Carrick
(1243–1304) (d.1292)

Isabel of Mar [1] = ROBERT I = [2] Elizabeth de Burgh
(d.1296) 'The Bruce' (d.1327)
1306–29

Siblings of Robert 'The Bruce'

Isabel c.1272–1358
Christina c.1278–1356/7
Nigel c.1279–1306
Edward c. 1280–1318
Mary c.1282–1323
Margaret (dates unknown)
Thomas c.1284–1307
Alexander c.1285–1307
Elizabeth (dates unknown)
Matilda (dates unknown)

Eleanor = John
Comyn
(d.1302)

JOHN (BALLIOL) = Isabel de Warenne
1292–96 (d.1313)

John Comyn
'The Red
Comyn' (d.1306)

Edward Balliol Henry Balliol
(d.1363) (d.1332)

Walter the Steward = Marjorie
(d.1326) (d.1316)

DAVID II = Joan
1329–71 (d.1362)

*The Stewart line of Kings and Queens of Scotland, and (from 1603) also England, lasted for more than 340 years, until 1714.

Elizabeth Mure [1] = ROBERT II (Stewart)* = [2] Euphemia, Countess
(d. before 1322) 1371–90 of Moray (d.1388/9)

The Golden Age of Alexander III

How Scotland fell from peace and prosperity to despair.

Alexander III succeeded his father as King of Scotland in 1249 when he was just eight years old. He reigned for 36 years.

The Great Seal of Alexander III (*c.*1249), which shows him as a knight on horseback, with a long coat covering a mail tunic, sword, and shield with a heraldic lion.

During his reign there was peace with England, because his wife, Queen Margaret, was a daughter of the English king, Henry III. There was also a truce at last with the dangerous Norsemen, when Alexander's daughter married the King of Norway.

But although it was a time of peace for many, to Alexander it brought great unhappiness. His wife died in 1275, and then his two sons.

Burghs

During the 13th century, many townships, called **burghs**, were founded as centres for trade. Weekly markets (such as the one illustrated, left) were held in the open space around the mercat cross. Merchants were required to call at the tolbooth to pay taxes on their goods. Inhabitants of the burgh, the **burgesses**, paid rent to the king and elected their own officials.

C0062 44053

National Museums Scotland

Wallace and Bruce
and the First War of Independence

Antony Kamm

with illustrations by Jennifer Campbell

SCOTTIES SERIES EDITORS
Frances and Gordon Jarvie

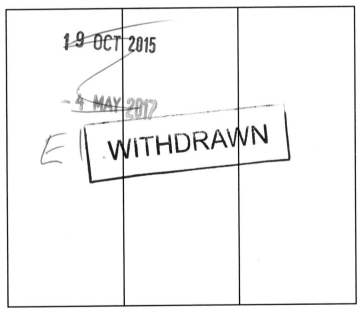

libraries

Ibrox Library
1 Midlock Street
Glasgow G51 1SL
Phone: 0141 276 0712 Fax 276 0713

This book is due for return on or before the last date shown below. It may be renewed by telephone, personal application, fax or post, quoting this date, author, title and the book number

19 OCT 2015

4 MAY 2017

WITHDRAWN

Glasgow Life and its service brands, including Glasgow Libraries, (found at www.glasgowlife.org.uk) are operating names for Culture and Sport Glasgow

...on Data

© NATIONAL MUSEUMS SCOTLAND
for pages 2 (Alexander III coins); 3 (David II coin); 4 (Alexander III seal); 6 (water image); 8 (seal); 9 (Ragman Roll seal); 21 (Charles I pendant; 24 (Robert Wishart, seal); 25 (Robert I, seal); 29 (Edinburgh Castle); 34 (Robert II coins); 39 (David II coin)

SCOTTIE BOOKS

Glasgow
CITY COUNCIL

FURTHER CREDITS ON PAGE viii OF ACTIVITY SECTION.

For a full listing of titles and related merchandise from NMS Enterprises Limited – Publishing:
www.nms.ac.uk/books

the author of this book has been asserted by him in accordance with the Copyright, Designs and Patents Act 1988.

© JENNIFER CAMPBELL 1996, 1997, 2015
black & white illustrations on pages 4, 5, 6, 8, 11, 12, 14, 16, 17, 18 (battle plan), 19, 20, 25, 26, 28, 30, 31 (including battle plan), 32, 33 (battle plan), 34, 37, 39

Genealogical Chart

OF THE SUCCESSION TO THE SCOTTISH THRONE 1124–1390

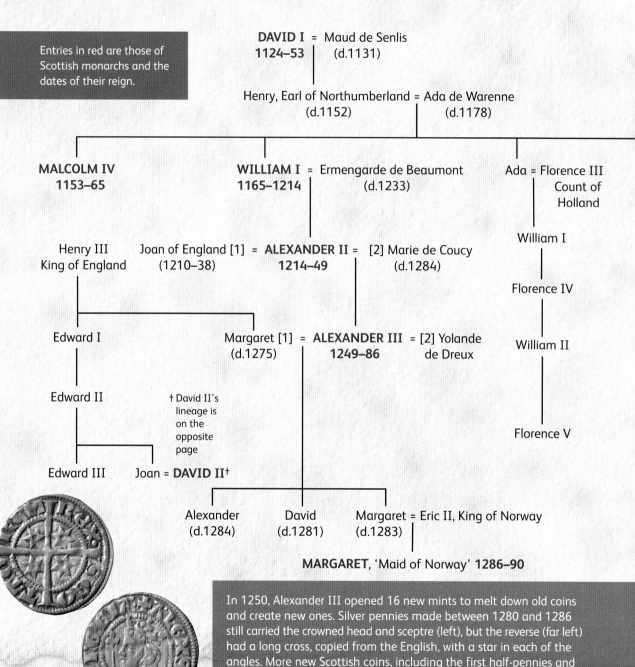

Entries in red are those of Scottish monarchs and the dates of their reign.

DAVID I = Maud de Senlis
1124–53 | (d.1131)

Henry, Earl of Northumberland = Ada de Warenne
(d.1152) | (d.1178)

MALCOLM IV
1153–65

WILLIAM I = Ermengarde de Beaumont
1165–1214 | (d.1233)

Ada = Florence III
| Count of
| Holland

Henry III
King of England

Joan of England [1] = **ALEXANDER II** = [2] Marie de Coucy
(1210–38) | **1214–49** | (d.1284)

William I

Edward I

Margaret [1] = **ALEXANDER III** = [2] Yolande
(d.1275) | **1249–86** | de Dreux

Florence IV

William II

Edward II

† David II's lineage is on the opposite page

Florence V

Edward III   Joan = **DAVID II**†

Alexander   David   Margaret = Eric II, King of Norway
(d.1284)   (d.1281)   (d.1283)

MARGARET, 'Maid of Norway' 1286–90

In 1250, Alexander III opened 16 new mints to melt down old coins and create new ones. Silver pennies made between 1280 and 1286 still carried the crowned head and sceptre (left), but the reverse (far left) had a long cross, copied from the English, with a star in each of the angles. More new Scottish coins, including the first half-pennies and farthings, were made in Alexander III's reign than at any other time in the Middle Ages.

There was now no male heir to succeed him. His daughter, Margaret, died after giving birth to a girl, also called Margaret. In 1285, hoping for a son, Alexander married the young Yolande de Dreux, daughter of a French count.

That year a rumour spread that the Day of Judgement was near, when the end of the world would come. One terrible night of storm, Alexander was at Edinburgh Castle, drinking with his lords after a council meeting. Suddenly he announced that he was going to ride home to the royal manor at Kinghorn, where Yolande was, 20 miles away on the other side of the Firth of Forth.

This Memorial to King Alexander III (1241–86) can be found in Kinghorn. It marks the place where his horse stumbled on the cliff-tops.

In dreadful weather, he crossed the Forth by the ferry to the burgh of Inverkeithing. In spite of the warnings of one of the leading burgesses, who met him when he landed and offered him hospitality for the night, the King insisted on continuing his journey and rode off ahead of his guides into the night.

The next day the king's body was found on the shore beneath a cliff. His only surviving heir was his three-year-old granddaughter, Margaret, the 'Maid of Norway'. The Day of Judgement had indeed arrived, for Alexander's death began the trail of events that led to the Wars of Independence.

The Guardians of Scotland

Death of a child-queen. How the new ruler of Scotland was chosen.

After the funeral of Alexander III, the leading men of Scotland met and appointed six 'Guardians of the Peace' (two earls, two bishops, two barons) to govern the country on behalf of their child-queen, Margaret.

When Margaret was six years old, the Guardians agreed to a proposal by Edward I, King of England, that she should marry his infant son, Edward of Caernarvon. Edward I was so keen to have Margaret in his power that he despatched a ship to Norway, filled with gifts and food delicacies, to fetch her to the wedding. Her father, the King of Norway, sent it back without her. He wanted Margaret to arrive on a Norwegian ship. Sadly, she died at Orkney, during the voyage.

There was now no rightful ruler of Scotland. Fourteen men applied for the post of king. Four had a claim, by birth, as descendants of David I (1124–53). They were John Balliol; the aged Robert Bruce, Lord of Annandale (known as 'The Competitor'); John Hastings (a Welshman); and Florence V, Count of Holland.

Who should rule?

The court that met to decide who should succeed to the Scottish throne consisted of 104 members – 24 nominated by Edward I, and 40 each by Balliol and Bruce, with Edward as chairman. For 18 months, with a few rest periods while ancient documents were searched for, they listened to the lawyers arguing the claims of the candidates, and deliberated among themselves.

Totally perplexed, the Guardians consulted Edward I. He set up a legal court, on Scottish soil, to consider the matter. When finally the court could not agree, Edward was invited to decide. He chose John Balliol, who in law had the strongest claim – a bad choice for Scotland, but a good one for Edward!

'Hammer of the Scots'

The war begins. Both sides commit atrocities. Balliol dithers while Edward marches.

King Edward I

The first thing that John Balliol did after being crowned king was swear homage to Edward I as his overlord. Though Balliol tried to be a just and effective ruler, Edward kept reminding him who was really in charge.

In 1294 Edward declared war on France and demanded that the Scottish king, with ten of his earls and 16 barons, should join his army. This was too much even for John Balliol who, with the support of his parliament, signed a treaty with France. This meant that the Scots were now at war with the English, and in 1296 a War for Independence began.

While John Balliol dithered and the Scots tried to organise their defences, Edward's army marched north from Newcastle and besieged Berwick. Seven Scottish earls crossed the border into Cumberland with a force of infantry. They burned villages, slaughtered men, stole cattle, and made an unsuccessful attack on Carlisle. Edward sacked Berwick with unbelievable cruelty and bloodshed.

John Balliol

* Born in 1249
* Crowned 30 November 1292
* Reigned for 4 years
* Married Isabel de Warenne
* Died in Normandy, April 1313

The above picture comes from a 16th-century book of heraldry, The Seton Armorial, which illustrates the coats-of-arms of Scottish kings. Why is John Balliol's royal sceptre broken, and his shield empty? Read about what happened to this unhappy king on page 8.

The Scots attack the north of England. How John Balliol got his nickname.

The Scottish earls made another expedition – into Northumberland this time. They destroyed churches and monasteries, as well as villages, and, it is said, burned alive 200 schoolboys at Corbridge.

Edward marched on Dunbar, whose defenders sent an anguished message for help to John Balliol. A Scottish army, sent to relieve the castle, charged against the disciplined English forces. They were defeated. That was the end of Scottish resistance for some time.

Tails, you win ...

When the Scots defending Dunbar Castle saw the Scottish army approaching the horizon, they jumped up and down, waved banners, and shouted insults at the besiegers below: 'Come and have your tails cut off, you English dogs!' (It was commonly believed in Scotland at that time that all Englishmen had tails.)

Between April and August 1296, Edward toured eastern and central Scotland, from Berwick to Elgin and back – more a triumphal march than a military campaign.

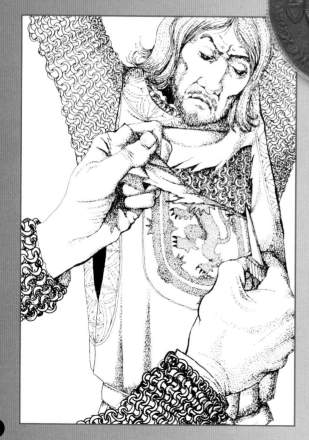

Edinburgh Castle surrendered after a week. As Edward's army approached Stirling, the defenders abandoned the castle, leaving the keys to be handed over by the janitor. Balliol was forced to confess that he had rebelled against his English overlord and had to give up his kingdom. His final humiliation came at Montrose, where in public the royal coat of arms was torn from his **tabard** (ceremonial coat). From this he earned the nickname 'Toom Tabard' ('Empty Coat'). He was then sent as a prisoner to England. In 1299 Edward released him into the care of the Pope. Until his death in 1313, Balliol lived in various stately houses in France.

On his way north, Edward had stopped at Perth, where he took the Stone of Destiny, on which for 450 years kings of Scotland had been crowned. (There is a legend that says it was stolen originally from the Irish!) Edward had the stone placed in Westminster Abbey, under the seat of a specially constructed coronation throne. There it remained for 700 years, and almost every king or queen of England and Great Britain since Edward I has been crowned upon it.

Having also ordered the Scottish royal treasure and many holy relics to be removed to London, Edward called a parliament in Berwick on 28 August 1296. Here leading Scots, who had not already done so, recorded their oath of loyalty to him as ruler of Scotland. They did this by adding their names to the **Ragman Roll**, so called because of the ragged appearance of its bottom part, to which many seals, such as the one below, were attached.

Among the names missing from the list were those of Malcolm Wallace of Elderslie, in Renfrewshire, and his younger brother, William.

King Edward I's tomb in Westminster Abbey.

Scottorum Malleus

Two hundred years after the death of Edward I, someone painted on his tomb this Latin inscription: 'Scottorum Malleus hic est, 1308. Pactum Serva.' This means, 'Here lies the Hammer of the Scots, 1308. Keep the Faith'. This is the first reference to the king's well-known nickname, but he may have been called it soon after his death, or even when still alive.

The Stone of Destiny

In 1950, the Stone of Destiny was stolen from Westminster Abbey by four Scottish students. The police tried, but failed, to find it. Three and a half months later, it was left in Arbroath Abbey, and returned to London. Do you know where it is now?

Answer on page 40

The Revenge of William Wallace

Left: A stained-glass window from the National Wallace Monument, Stirling. One of 11 windows, it was installed in 1885, 16 years after the building was opened.

Many of the legends and stories of William Wallace first appear in a long poem describing his deeds and adventures. It was written about 170 years after Wallace's death by Harry the Minstrel, also known as Blind Harry. Some of the episodes in it became the basis of the film *Braveheart* (1995).

Who was William Wallace? And why did he carry out his campaign of violence?

William was born in about 1274. The exact year is not known, nor anything for certain about his childhood and youth. His father was probably the Alan Wallace recorded as having paid rent to the crown for land in Ayrshire. William had two brothers, Malcolm and John.

We do know that in May 1297 he killed William Heselrig, Sheriff of Lanark, an unpopular Englishman who was in the town to preside over the local assizes (courts).

According to one story, which owes more to legend than to truth, Wallace had a wealthy girlfriend in Lanark, Marion Braidfute. He used to visit her secretly after he had been involved in some trouble. One night he was spotted by English soldiers, who pursued him to Marion's house. She let Wallace out the back door and refused to allow the soldiers to enter until he had escaped.

Heselrig was so angry it is thought that he either murdered Marion himself or had her murdered, and then burned her house to the ground. It is more likely that Wallace simply chose the place, the occasion, and the victim, as most fully representing the hated English authority over the Scots. Whatever the reason, his killing of Heselrig was the signal for Scots to rebel against the English, and to regard Wallace as their leader.

For his act of violence at Lanark, Wallace was made an outlaw. He was hunted by the English, but instead of going into hiding he went out after them.

His first target was an English judge at Scone, 80 miles from Lanark. He and his band of armed men rode there on horses, probably provided by Sir William Douglas who had been Governor of Berwick when it was sacked by Edward I. Like Wallace, Douglas wanted revenge. The judge managed to escape just before Wallace and Douglas arrived, but he left behind treasure, which the Scots took.

When the people of Scotland heard about the raid on Scone, they started their own rebellions. The English lords retreated into their castles and were difficult to dislodge. In fury the Scots took revenge on innocent English people, even priests and women.

Blind Harry

Before printing came to Scotland in 1508, books were written out by hand. The extract (below) from the Scots poet Blind Harry is the only surviving written version from his own time. It was taken down by Prior John Ramsay of Perth in 1488. The side-heading in the margin reads: *'How Wallace slew* [the] *tresorar* [treasurer] *of Ingland* [at] *the bryig* [bridge] *of* [Ste]*rling.'*

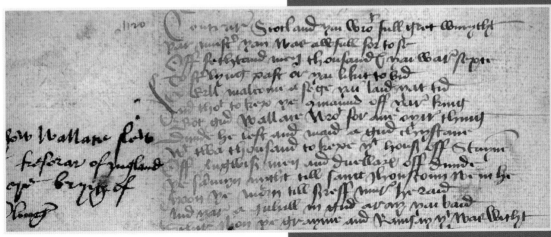

July 1297. Wallace is ranging the countryside with his growing band of followers.

While Wallace was in the east, an English army came up against a Scottish force at Irvine. The Scots surrendered without a fight, but, it is said, cleverly prolonged the talking to give Wallace time to raise a bigger army.

There are many stories told about what Wallace was doing during July. Blind Harry tells us that he stormed the sea-girt fortress of Dunnottar Castle, by Stonehaven, and burned its defenders to death in the chapel; that he then marched to Aberdeen, where he destroyed a hundred English ships. If you

Dunnottar Castle, built in the 7th century, gets its name from the Scottish Gaelic word *Dùn Fhoithear*, 'fort on the shelving slope'. It stands on a steep headland, overlooking the North Sea, two miles south of Stonehaven, Aberdeenshire.

look at the map opposite, you will see that the distance makes this improbable. It is more likely that, starting from his headquarters in Selkirk Forest, he was clearing the English out of Perthshire and Fife by force.

More and more Scots were joining Wallace. The chief of these was Andrew Murray, who brought his own infantry and cavalry. He assumed joint command with Wallace. Murray had already seized most of the English-held castles in the north of Scotland.

Wallace was besieging Dundee Castle when he heard that a fresh English army was marching towards Stirling. He left the siege in the hands of the townspeople of Dundee, and rode to Stirling with all haste.

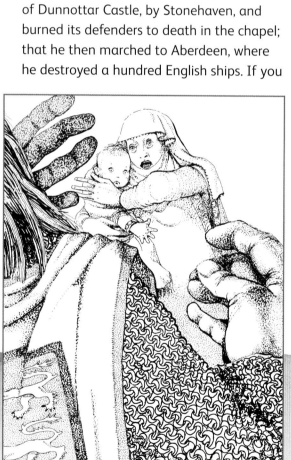

Babe in Arms

There was so much hatred between the English and Scots that Edward I ordered that all land in England belonging to Scots should be seized, and all Scots found in England should be arrested as dangerous. One of those arrested was a son of William Douglas. He was only one year old!

Principal routes in Scotland (often no more than tracks, sometimes following old Roman roads.

— — — Border
F ········· Ferry
X Battles

0 MILES 80

ORKNEY

OUTER ISLES

BATTLES X
1 Stirling Bridge 1297
2 Falkirk 1298
3 Methven 1306
4 Dalry 1306
5 Loudoun Hill 1307
6 Inverurie 1307
7 Pass of Brander 1308
8 Bannockburn 1314
9 Scawton Moor 1322
10 Dupplin 1332
11 Halidon Hill 1333
12 Neville's Cross 1346

Kinloss Abbey
Elgin
MORAY
BUCHAN
6
Kildrummy Castle
Aberdeen
Brechin Castle
Dunnottar Castle
Montrose
HEBRIDES
Arbroath
4
Scone
7
3
Dundee
10
St Andrews
Perth
FIFE
Bothwell Castle
Stirling
Dunfermline
Kinghorn
1 8
FIRTH OF FORTH
Cardross
2
F
Dunbar
Glasgow
Linlithgow
Edinburgh
11
Berwick
ARGYLL
Elderslie
5
Lanark
LOTHIAN
Roxburgh
FIRTH OF CLYDE
Irvine
Melrose
Ayr
KYLE
Douglas
Selkirk
Norham Castle
Rathlin
Turnberry Castle
CARRICK
ANNANDALE
NORTHUMBERLAND
Girvan
Newcastle
Dumfries
Lanercost
Corbridge
IRELAND
GALLOWAY
F
Carlisle
Whithorn
CUMBERLAND
DURHAM
12
Cockermouth
Stanhope Park
Rievaulx Abbey and York
9

The Battle of Stirling Bridge

How the English army fell into Wallace's trap.

Although at the time of the Wars of Independence, Stirling Castle consisted mainly of wooden buildings and fencing, it was still regarded as the strongest fortress in Scotland. It held a vital position overlooking the bridge and the fords over the river Forth. Whoever held the castle commanded the main route to the north of Scotland (see map, page 13), and it had

been held by the English since it capitulated to Edward I the previous year.

The English army was camped under the rocky crag, on top of which was the castle. The bridge over the Forth was only just wide enough to allow horsemen to cross in pairs.

Wallace and Murray drew up their army just over a mile beyond the bridge on Abbey Craig, an outcrop of the Ochil Hills.

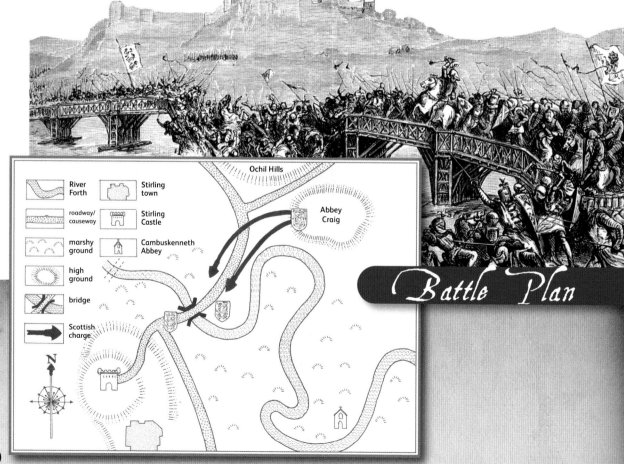

Battle Plan

Legend:
- River Forth
- roadway/ causeway
- marshy ground
- high ground
- bridge
- Scottish charge
- Stirling town
- Stirling Castle
- Cambuskenneth Abbey

Ochil Hills

Abbey Craig

N

Between the bridge and Abbey Craig ran a narrow causeway over marshy ground, on which it would be difficult for the English cavalry to manoeuvre. And in the battle the Scots only used foot-soldiers, many of whom were armed with fearsome spears, four metres long.

Early in the morning of 11 September 1297, the vanguard of the English army began to advance, two by two, across the bridge. They were then recalled because their commander, the elderly Earl of Surrey, had overslept. But now alert, Surrey sent two friars to invite Wallace to surrender. Wallace, however, sent them back with his answer: 'We are not here to make peace, but to fight for our country's freedom. Let the English come on: we'll meet them beard to beard.'

As the Scots kept to their ranks and waited, the English began to cross the bridge again. When about half were over, Wallace sounded his horn. The entire Scottish army came charging down the hill. Five thousand English cavalry and infantry were now trapped in a loop in the river. Surrey and the rest of his force could only watch in horror at the slaughter of their comrades, many of whom were pushed into the river and drowned.

When Surrey saw the day was lost, he was so desperate to escape that he rode to Berwick without any stops to feed his horse, which collapsed under him on arrival. He left Stirling Castle in the care of Sir Marmaduke Tweng, who had fought his way back through the Scottish host and over the bridge again.

The chief Englishman to die was Hugh Cressingham, Edward I's treasurer and tax-collector in Scotland. After the battle, the skin was torn from his body and cut into pieces, which people kept as tokens of Scottish free-dom from the hated rule he represented. Cressingham was a fat man, and there was enough skin left over for Wallace to have a swordbelt made for himself.

A modern-day aerial view of the Stirling Bridge area.

Sir William Wallace

How Wallace took over the government of Scotland, punished the English, and prepared for the next battle.

When Stirling Castle surrendered soon after the battle because of lack of provisions, Wallace spared the life of its commander, Tweng, because of his bravery in the field. Wallace also took the towns of Edinburgh, Roxburgh and Berwick from the English, and burned others south of the river Forth.

Then he and Andrew Murray, both still in their early twenties, took in hand the government of Scotland. In the name of their absent king – John Balliol, still imprisoned in England – they wrote to merchants in German ports encouraging the reopening of trade between the two countries, now that Scotland had been freed from the English. They signed themselves 'Commanders of the army of the kingdom of Scotland and the community of that realm'.

Murray died a few weeks later of a wound received at the Battle of Stirling Bridge.

Wallace, responding to the popular feeling that the English should be punished, led an expedition into England.

Since he had no siege weapons with which to subdue castles or take fortified towns, the ordinary people of the countryside, and the monks and priests of the monasteries and abbeys, suffered most from Wallace's fury. He led his wild Scottish soldiers killing and looting right across the land as far as Cocker-mouth in the west and Newcastle in the east. But when he tried to invade Durham, he was faced with blizzards of snow and ice never witnessed before in those parts.

Stirling Castle today.

Bishop Fraser of St Andrews, one of the original Guardians, died in 1297. Wallace sent orders from England that his successor as bishop should be William Lamberton, a man equally devoted to the cause of an independent Scotland. Lamberton courageously travelled through seas patrolled by English ships to the Continent, and overland to Rome, to be consecrated by the Pope.

In the face of bad weather, Wallace's men, weighed down with booty, declared they had had enough. They believed that St Cuthbert, the patron saint of Durham, was protecting his people by inflicting such terrible storms.

Shortly after Wallace returned from England at the head of his army, the Scots awarded him two honours. He was made a knight (Sir William Wallace), and elected sole Guardian of Scotland. As Guardian, he had not only to supervise the whole government of the country in the absence of John Balliol, but also to prepare for the next onslaught from Edward I. It was not long coming.

This time Edward was determined that nothing should go wrong, however long it took. He made York, half-way between London and Edinburgh, the headquarters of his government. He ordered his army, which included 10,000 heavy armoured cavalry, to meet him at Roxburgh in June 1298. Then, for a month, with food stocks getting low, the English hunted for the Scottish army.

At Linlithgow, Edward decided that he had no choice but to retreat to Edinburgh and possibly to abandon the campaign. Just then,

he received a report from two Scottish earls, who were faithful to the English cause, that Wallace and his army were encamped 18 miles away, near Falkirk.

Wallace was possibly as surprised to find the English advancing against his position as Edward was to have discovered his enemy at last. In the months since the Battle of Stirling Bridge, however, Wallace had trained his peasant army in new tactics.

Fast Fact

The night before the battle at Falkirk, Edward was so concerned that Wallace might launch a surprise attack he ordered his men to lie down beside their horses. During the night his own horse trod on him, breaking several ribs. The English were in such a state of alarm that news of his injury caused panic in their ranks.

Falkirk (1298) and after

The battle is lost, and Wallace is on the run.

Wallace's position was on the slope of a hill, with an area of boggy ground in front, where two burns met. He arranged his spearmen in four huge, circular, human fortresses, called **schiltrons**. Between the schiltrons he placed his archers, with their short-range bows. Behind them was the Scottish cavalry, whose job it was to ride down the English bowmen.

The English had not eaten for 24 hours. Edward wanted them to wait for breakfast, but was outvoted by his cavalry commanders. They rode at the Scottish line, swinging out to each side when they met the bog.

The Scottish horsemen turned and fled. Almost all the Scottish archers died in that first attack, but the schiltrons held firm against several assaults.

Edward ordered his cavalry to withdraw. Then he unleashed his secret weapon – the longbowmen from Sherwood forest and Wales, backed up by Continental mercenaries armed with crossbows.

Bothwell Castle (opposite page) commanded the route from northern Scotland to the south west (see map page 13). Its owner, who was being cared for elsewhere, was three-year-old Andrew Murray, son of Wallace's commander. In 1301 Edward besieged the castle with 6800 men and an awesome siege-tower, specially constructed in Glasgow and brought into place on 30 wagons. The castle capitulated after about three weeks.

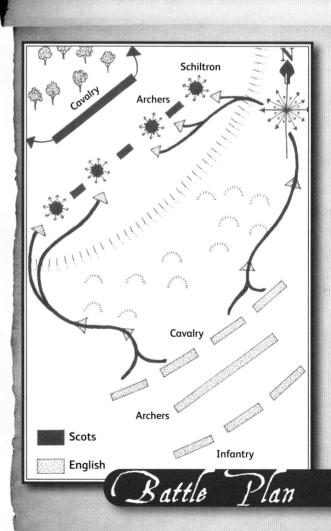

Schiltron
Cavalry
Archers
N
Cavalry
Archers
Infantry
Scots
English

Battle Plan

18

From long range, with no Scottish cavalry to oppose them, they picked off man after man in the schiltrons, until it was safe for the cavalry to go in and finish off the rest.

Wallace escaped. As long as he was alive, Edward could not rest. Though Wallace resigned as Guardian and went abroad for a time, Scottish resistance continued.

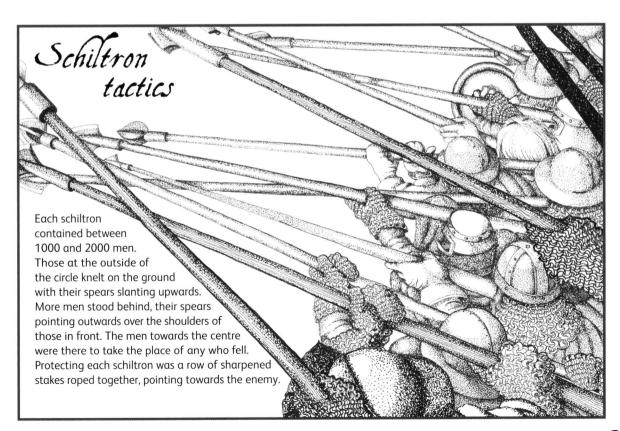

Schiltron tactics

Each schiltron contained between 1000 and 2000 men. Those at the outside of the circle knelt on the ground with their spears slanting upwards. More men stood behind, their spears pointing outwards over the shoulders of those in front. The men towards the centre were there to take the place of any who fell. Protecting each schiltron was a row of sharpened stakes roped together, pointing towards the enemy.

The Scots surrender

After campaigning in Galloway in 1300, and in south-west Scotland in 1301, Edward I, accompanied by Edward of Caernarvon (now Prince of Wales), launched a full-scale invasion in 1303.

Wallace's final betrayal.

The king had three enormous floating pontoon bridges constructed off the east coast of England at King's Lynn. These were transported by sea to the Firth of Forth, so that his men could cross over on them direct into Fife. On his way north he met serious opposition only at Brechin Castle, which Edward subdued with siege engines brought by sea to Montrose. Having progressed as far as Kinloss Abbey in Morayshire, he returned to Dunfermline for the winter.

In February 1304, representatives of the Scottish nobles formally surrendered to Edward. He promised in return that under his rule the Scots would have the same rights they had during the reign of Alexander III. The nobles did not include Sir John de Soules, the senior of the Guardians who had taken over from Wallace, nor Wallace himself.

Edward had only two pieces of unfinished business left. He destroyed Stirling Castle, which its commander claimed had been entrusted to him personally by Sir John. And he continued relentlessly to pursue Wallace.

To batter Stirling Castle into submission, Edward used 13 vast siege engines, backed up by explosive devices. The defenders held out for three months, surrendering only because they were starving. Even then, Edward insisted on an extra day's bombardment to try out his new weapon, the War-Wolf. Edward's queen and her ladies watched the War-Wolf in action from a window specially built into a house in the town.

Wallace was betrayed in Glasgow in August 1305, captured and taken in chains to London. In Westminster Hall he was accused of a multitude of crimes beginning with the murder of Heselrig, and of being a traitor to Edward I. He was convicted without defence and sentenced to a peculiarly nasty death.

Wallace was taken straight out, bound to a hurdle and dragged by horses through the streets to the gallows. There he was hanged and, for his treason, cut down while still alive and his bowels torn out and burned. His head was cut off and set up on London Bridge. His trunk was chopped into four pieces, which were sent to Newcastle, Berwick, Perth and Stirling to be displayed in public.

In the eyes of the English, Wallace may have been a criminal, but he was not a traitor, for he never put his name to the Ragman Roll.

The Scots had surrendered. Wallace was now dead, but the War raged on.

Westminster Hall

Until 1882, the Law Courts of England were centred on Westminster Hall. In addition to Wallace and King Charles I (see above), other famous people were tried there. Can you unscramble the names of two of them below:

ISR MSATOH ROEM (in 1535)
YUG WKAFSE (1606)

Answers on page 40

Death of Wallace

Robert the Bruce

His upbringing and loyalties. Why he sided with Edward I. And how the Red Comyn was murdered.

Although the origins of Turnberry Castle are unknown, in the late 13th century it belonged to Marjorie, Countess of Carrick. Although it is not known whether the castle is the actual birth-place of Bruce, it is a fact that he spent his boy-hood living in the castle.

Robert Bruce, generally known as Robert the Bruce, was probably born at Turnberry Castle. He was the grandson of Robert Bruce, 'The Competitor', second husband of Marjorie, Countess of Carrick in her own right.

Robert was the eldest of eleven children. He became Earl of Carrick in 1292 when his father resigned the title on being named by *his* father as successor to the Bruce claim to the throne of Scotland.

Fast fact

Robert the Bruce was brought up in a society that valued fighting skills above all. When there were no wars to fight, knights travelled around Europe taking part in tournaments. Bruce was regarded as one of the three most accomplished knights in the Christian world. The others were Henry of Luxembourg, later Holy Roman Emperor, and the English Sir Giles d'Argentine, who was to distinguish himself at the Battle of Bannockburn.

During the earlier part of the Wars of Independence, Robert the Bruce was some-times on one side, sometimes on the other. We should not be surprised that he and his family signed the Ragman Roll: not to have done so would have meant that they sup-ported John Balliol, to whose throne they felt they had a stronger claim. At the begin-ning of Wallace's first campaign, however, Bruce led out the men of Carrick in revolt against English rule.

In 1295 Robert the Bruce married Isabel, daughter of the Earl of Mar. She died the following year, having given birth to a daughter, Marjorie.

After William Wallace resigned as Guardian in 1298, Bruce was appointed joint Guardian with the hot-tempered John Comyn, Lord of Badenoch (known as the Red Comyn). The following year a third Guardian, Bishop Lamberton, was appointed. Bruce resigned from this post in 1300.

In 1302 Bruce was once more in league with the English. A document survives in which Edward I guarantees freedom and safety to Bruce, his followers and tenants, and gives him permanent possession of the lands of Carrick. He also undertook to support Bruce in any lawsuit against John Balliol, should Balliol, or Balliol's son and heir, try to reclaim the throne of Scotland. In return Bruce promised his good behaviour.

But Bruce needed Edward's support for another reason. He had fallen in love with Elizabeth de Burgh, daughter of the Earl of Ulster and one of Edward's chief supporters. They were married shortly after the terms of the document were agreed.

When the Scottish nobles surrendered to Edward I in 1304 (see page 20), it was the Red Comyn who conducted the negotiations. What happened next, however, was not what Edward, or anyone else for that matter, expected. After private talks with Bishop Lamberton, Bruce arranged a secret meeting with Comyn in Greyfriars Kirk in Dumfries in February 1306.

Nobody knows what they said to each other. It is most likely that Bruce asked Comyn to support him in a bid for the Scottish throne, and Comyn (whose mother was a sister of John Balliol) hotly refused. Whatever was said, Bruce stabbed Comyn with his dagger, and his followers dashed in to finish Comyn off with their swords. It was an act of murder. But it was also sacrilege, for the killing was done in a church.

A plaque at Greyfriars Kirk, Dumfries, that shows the spot where Bruce killed Comyn.

Sweetheart Abbey

Sweetheart Abbey was founded in 1273 by Balliol's mother, **Lady Dervorguilla of Galloway**, in memory of her husband John Balliol of Barnard Castle. On her death, she was laid to rest next to her husband's embalmed heart and the monks named their abbey in memory of her.

King of Scotland

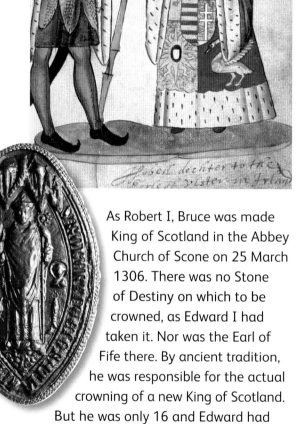

How Bruce made his peace with the Scottish Church. How he was crowned King. And how his womenfolk were treated by Edward I.

Bruce's first act after the murder of Comyn was to seize the castles in and around Dumfries. He also ensured that most of the castles guarding the entrance to the Firth of Clyde were under his control, so that he could obtain supplies and troops from Ireland and the Outer Isles.

Then he made his peace with the Bishop of Glasgow, Robert Wishart, in whose diocese Comyn had been murdered. Wishart not only forgave him, but provided robes fit for a king to wear, and a banner bearing the royal arms of Scotland. In return Bruce promised to uphold the liberties of the Scottish Church and to govern with its assent.

Bruce then sent a message to Bishop Lamberton in Berwick, inviting him to Scone for the coronation.

As Robert I, Bruce was made King of Scotland in the Abbey Church of Scone on 25 March 1306. There was no Stone of Destiny on which to be crowned, as Edward I had taken it. Nor was the Earl of Fife there. By ancient tradition, he was responsible for the actual crowning of a new King of Scotland. But he was only 16 and Edward had forbidden him to attend.

Above, left: Seal of Robert Wishart, Bishop of Glasgow.

Above: Bruce and his second wife, Elizabeth de Burgh. This image is from The Seton Armorial, a book of heraldry created for Robert, 6th Lord Seton (see also page 7).

In his place, the Earl's aunt, Isabella of Fife, Countess of Buchan, crowned Bruce with a gold coronet. Although she was married to the Earl of Buchan, who was an ally of Edward I and a relative of the Red Comyn, she insisted on taking part in the ceremony. She even rode there on one of her husband's best war-horses, without his knowledge.

Bruce crowned King of Scotland

An impression of the reverse of the First Great Seal of Robert I (Bruce) of Scotland, *c.*1306. The king is shown as a knight on horseback.

Although Bruce was now King of Scotland, Edward held all the cards! He appointed Aymer de Valence, a brother-in-law of the murdered Comyn, as special commissioner in Scotland, with orders to show no mercy. Meanwhile, Bruce was here and there, seizing castles and quelling uprisings. Even bishops Lamberton and the elderly Wishart played fighting parts, until they were captured, sent to England, and clapped in irons in dungeons.

Bruce's attempt to bring de Valence to battle was a disaster, and at Methven his troops were surprised and routed. Bruce covered the retreat from the rear, encouraging survivors and fighting off those in pursuit. Then he faced another defeat, at Dalry, near Tyndrum. This time, Bruce's party was ambushed by the Macdougalls of Argyll, kinsmen of the Red Comyn. As Bruce fought off a swarm of clansmen, one of them, it is said, got close enough to pull the brooch from the king's cloak before being cut down.

Bruce now sent for the women-folk of his family.

Bruce sent his wife Elizabeth, his daughter Marjorie, his sister Mary, Isabel the Countess of Buchan, and other women, to Kildrummy Castle, near Aberdeen, under the protection of his brother Nigel. Then he took a boat to Rathlin, a tiny island off the Irish coast. No one knows where he went from there.

Legend has it ...

When Bruce was forced to flee Scotland, he is said to have hidden in a cave on Rathlin Island, off the Irish coast. Lying awake one night, he saw a spider hanging by its thread. Six times it tried and failed to reach the wall. When it succeeded on the seventh attempt, Bruce took heart. He would try and try again, until he recovered his kingdom.

In February 1307, when he slipped back into Carrick, all was gloom and despair. His earldom of Carrick had been confiscated by Edward, and Bruce's former tenants were too frightened to come out in support of him.

Kildrummy Castle had fallen and Nigel Bruce had been hanged, drawn and quartered. The ladies were forced to flee and made it as far as the sanctuary of St Duthac at Tain in Easter Ross. There they were captured by a Balliol supporter, Earl William of Ross, who handed them over to Edward I's men.

Bruce's young Queen was only 17 and as Elizabeth's father was a close friend of Edward he treated her slightly better than some of his enemies, placing her under strict house arrest in England. She was moved around the country – Burstwick, Bisham Manor, Windsor Castle, Shaftesbury Abbey, Barking Abbey and Rochester Castle – until her release (see page 34) in 1314. Bruce's daughter Marjorie was sent to Watton Priory, a nunnery, until her release, also in 1314.

Bruce's brothers – Alexander, Dean of Glasgow, and Thomas – whom he had sent ahead with an expeditionary force of 18 ships, had been captured, hanged and beheaded. All Bruce had now were a few loyal companions, 40 mounted men provided by a female cousin, Christian of Carrick, and his own strength of character.

Punishment enough ...

However, for the brave Countess of Buchan and Mary Bruce, Edward devised a most humiliating punishment. Each one was shut up in a cage jutting out from the castle wall of Berwick and Roxburgh respectively. Food and drink were handed in to them and they were only allowed to retire behind the wall to use the lavatory.

The return of the King

How Bruce slowly regained the upper hand. The death of the 'Hammer of the Scots'. The final trial of strength.

Loudoun Hill

Bruce realised that his only hope lay in guerrilla warfare – outwitting and surprising his enemies. Not only did the English want him dead, but also Scots who still supported the cause of John Balliol, or who wanted revenge for the murder of the Red Comyn. There are many stories of Bruce's narrow escapes and of his skill in hand-to-hand fights with men who had been sent to kill him.

In May 1307 Bruce managed to manoeuvre Aymer de Valence into fighting a battle in an enclosed space at Loudoun Hill, where his spearmen defeated and routed the English cavalry. Three days later his tiny army scattered a force under the Earl of Gloucester, and chased him back to Ayr.

This was too much for Edward I, who was lying sick and tired at Lanercost Priory, near Carlisle. He rose from his bed, had himself placed in a litter at the head of his army, and set out for Scotland. He had only gone a few miles when he died, at Burgh-on-Sands. He is said to have given instructions that his bones should be carried in an urn in front of the army until the Scots were finally defeated. If he did so, his son, now Edward II, who hated fighting, took no notice. He buried his father, bones and all, in Westminster Abbey.

The Augustinian priory at Lanercost was founded by Robert de Vaux between 1165 and 1174. It suffered frequent attacks during the Anglo-Scottish wars, once by Robert Bruce himself. It was here that Edward I rested, before leaving in pursuit of Bruce's army, only to die a few miles up the road. Although there is evidence of the original building, the east end is the earliest surviving part of the church and dates to the 13th century.

Bruce could now concentrate on his Scottish enemies, including the Earl of Buchan and the Macdougall family.

But he was ill on his way to fight the Earl of Buchan, and when the two forces met at Inverurie, he had to be supported on his horse by a man on each side. At the mere sight of him, the Earl's troops dispersed. Bruce's subsequent treatment of the lands and people of Buchan was so violent that it became known as the 'herschip [ravaging] of Buchan'.

At the Pass of Brander, Bruce beat the Macdougalls at their own game. The track was narrow – on one side was a steep drop down into Loch Awe, and on the other the steep slope of Ben Cruachan.

The Macdougalls were waiting in ambush for him above the track. But, unknown to them, Bruce had sent Sir James Douglas (the Black Douglas) with a party of bow-men and experienced guerrilla fighters by a roundabout route to a point higher up the mountain. When the Macdougalls began their assault, they were attacked not only from behind, but also by their intended victims, who came at them up the slope.

At Robert I's first parliament, the Scottish magnates drew up a letter to King Philip IV of France in response to his request for assistance in a crusade. The Scots replied expressing their support for Bruce as king, reminding Philip about Scotland's devastation by war, and promised help when peace was achieved.

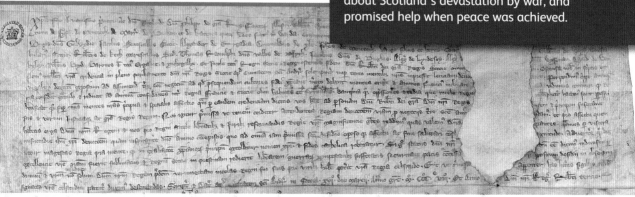

A letter to the French king by the magnates of Scotland regarding the right of King Robert I to the Crown of Scotland, 16 March 1309

After this victory Bruce felt sufficiently confident to hold his first parliament, at St Andrews in March 1309.

There was still the problem of the English-held fortifications. In 1313, seven years after Bruce had been proclaimed King of Scotland, 21 Scottish towns and castles were still in English hands. He had neither the siege engines to destroy them nor the time or resources to starve them into submission. However several attacks were planned against major strongholds.

PERTH: Bruce himself commanded the night assault on the town of Perth in January 1313. At the head of his men, he waded through the icy waters of the moat, which came up to his chin, carrying a rope ladder. When all the ladders were in position, he was the second man to reach the top of the wall. The town gave in without a fight.

ROXBURGH: James Douglas and his men crawled up to Roxburgh Castle at the dead of night and climbed the walls with rope ladders, catching the English by surprise. The castle was then destroyed. It is said that the English thought Douglas's men crawling up to the castle covered with cloaks were cattle.

EDINBURGH: While some of the force sent against Edinburgh Castle made a noisy diversion, the assault party clambered up the precipice on the other side. Led by Thomas Randolph, 1st Earl of Moray, they were guided by William Francis, who knew the way very well indeed. As a youth, he used to climb down the precipice to visit his girlfriend in the town and then back up again. Randolph's men took control and the castle's defences were destroyed.

STIRLING: In 1313, Edward Bruce, Robert's only surviving brother, who had besieged the strategically vital Stirling Castle without success, agreed an extraordinary pact with its commander. If no relieving English army came within three miles of Stirling before Midsummer's Day (24 June) 1314, the castle would surrender without a fight.

This was a challenge which even the peace-loving Edward II could not honourably ignore. He prepared his army not just to relieve the castle, but to crush the Scots for good. The last thing Bruce wanted, with his small, lightly-armed force, was a full-scale battle. Now he had no choice …

Detective work

When Bruce's men took control of enemy castles they destroyed them or their defences. Can you work out why this seemed a good idea?

Answer on page 40

Edinburgh Castle

The Battle of Bannockburn

Below: Camouflaged pits were dug into the ground, across which Bruce guessed the enemy would attack. **Calthrops** (upturned spikes) were spread over it, to deter the English cavalry.

DAY 1: The two armies. Setback for the English. Bruce's plan.

On 23 June 1314, one day before the deadline, Edward II led his army along the road from Falkirk to Stirling. He had 2000 heavy cavalry and 17,000 archers and foot-soldiers. A baggage train of over 200 wagons carried his army's food, supplies and pay.

Against this, Bruce had 500 light cavalry commanded by Sir Robert Keith, and about 5000 spearmen in four divisions, roughly according to which part of Scotland they came from. The divisional commanders were the Earl of Moray, James Douglas (who was knighted the previous evening), Edward Bruce, and the king himself.

Learning from the Battle of Falkirk, Bruce put only 500 men into each schiltron, and trained them to advance in step, like huge moving tanks bristling with spears. He also had in reserve 2000 'small people', mainly farmers, townsmen, craftsmen and labourers, keen but untrained in war. Each man carried whatever weapons he possessed.

Edward planned a frontal assault from the south, with 1500 cavalry and infantry under the Earl of Gloucester. At the same time, Sir Robert Clifford would lead a cavalry force round and behind the Scots, to get between them and Stirling Castle, attacking from the rear.

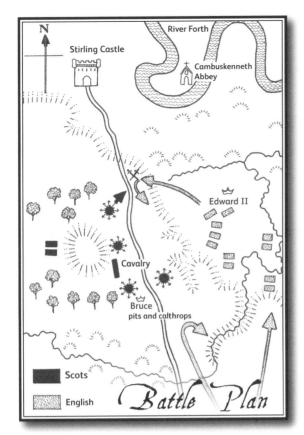

Battle Plan

Map labels:
N
River Forth
Stirling Castle
Cambuskenneth Abbey
Edward II
Cavalry
Bruce
pits and calthrops
Scots
English

That was the end of fighting for the day. At about 3 pm, Edward called a council of war. In spite of advice that the army should stay where it was, Edward insisted on crossing the Bannock Burn with all his knights and soldiers to a point east of the Scottish position. The morale of the English was low, especially as they had now to spend the night without the means of making a camp.

It was Bruce's turn to plan an attack. Edward did not think he would dare to do this, such was the difference in numbers between the two armies. But Bruce still had problems to solve. During the night the Earl of Atholl was meant to be marching to help Bruce. Instead, because of a row between the two families, he treacherously attacked the Scottish supply base at Cambuskenneth Abbey, killing its commander and his men.

The battle was almost over before it had begun. Bruce, without armour and mounted on a Highland pony to keep his war-horse fresh for battle, was inspecting his forward divisions when an enemy patrol crossed the burn. An English knight, Sir Henry de Bohun, recognising Bruce by the coronet round his helmet, lowered his lance and charged at him at full gallop. Bruce made his pony skip aside at the last moment and, as de Bohun thundered past, he split the Englishman's helmet with one blow of his battle-axe.

When the battle did start, Gloucester's force met the pits, the calthrops and the advancing schiltrons, and retreated in confusion. Clifford too was among the many casualties of the spears of Moray's single mobile schiltron, which lost only one man.

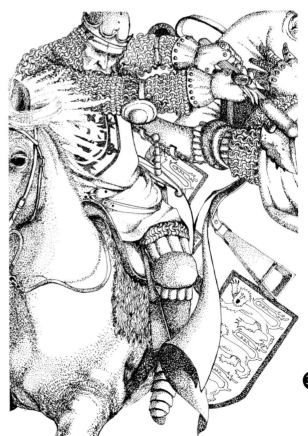

DAY 2: The Scots advance. The battle's turning point. Enter the 'small folk'.

It was a fine, dry morning. The divisions led by Edward Bruce, Moray and Douglas, with the king's division massed behind them, advanced down on to the plain to within a few hundred metres of the English front line. There they knelt down in prayer.

'Ha!' Edward II is reported to have said. 'They kneel for mercy.'

'They are kneeling for mercy, but not from your Majesty,' observed a courtier drily. 'I think they are about to attack!'

Edward II

The English trumpets sounding the alarm came as such a surprise that Gloucester had no time to pull on his protective outer coat before leading his cavalry against the advancing Scots. He died, pierced by several spears.

The Scottish spearmen fought, closely locked together, in one line now, advancing as an enormous, elongated, flexible schiltron.

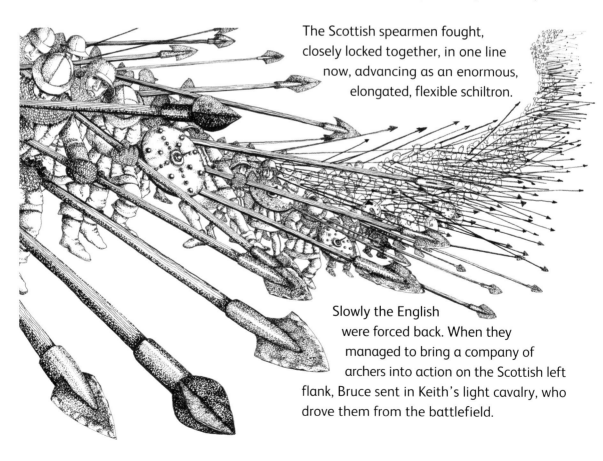

Slowly the English were forced back. When they managed to bring a company of archers into action on the Scottish left flank, Bruce sent in Keith's light cavalry, who drove them from the battlefield.

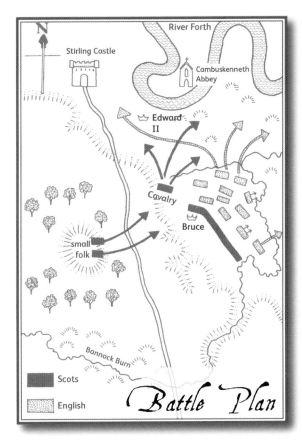

Battle Plan

N

Stirling Castle

River Forth

Cambuskenneth Abbey

Edward II

Cavalry

Bruce

small folk

Bannock Burn

Scots

English

Meanwhile the 'small folk', waiting in the rear of the battle, either on Bruce's orders or from sheer excitement, came racing in a body down the hill. The English, mistaking them for fully-armed reserves, turned and fled. Everywhere they were pursued. Some were drowned in the Forth; some in the evil waters of the Bannock Burn; others were cut down and butchered.

The Scots now descended on the English supply wagons, which contained treasure as well as money. It has been estimated that the loot they took that day would be worth over £50 million now.

It was a complete victory. English tactics had been appalling. Bruce, however, had trained his much smaller and less well-equipped army with the greatest skill, and led it with flair and a deep understanding of warfare.

Then Bruce brought his own division into the line. This was the turning point of the battle. The fierce Highlanders under Angus Og, Chief of the Macdonalds of the Isles, tore into the English line, causing utter confusion. Edward, realising that the battle was lost, was persuaded by Sir Giles d'Argentine to leave the field.

Having seen Edward on his way to safety, d'Argentine returned to the battle and charged to his death on the Scottish spears. Edward had been advised not to take refuge in Stirling Castle, where he faced certain capture. Instead, pursued all the way, he rode to Dunbar. From there he was taken in a small rowing boat to Berwick.

As for Angus Og, Bruce regarded his service, and that of his clan, so highly that the Macdonalds thereafter claimed the honour of fighting on the right flank of the front line.

This famous statue of Robert the Bruce, created by the sculptor Pilkington Jackson, stands near the Bannockburn Heritage Centre. It was unveiled in 1964.

After Bannockburn

Both Edward II and the Pope refuse to recognise the King of Scotland. The people of Scotland take a hand. And what is the 'Black Parliament'?

There was now an exchange of prisoners. For the Earl of Hereford, Bruce got back his Queen, daughter Marjorie, sister Mary, and Bishop Wishart, now blind. Bishop Lamberton had been allowed to return to Scotland in 1309, and the Countess of Buchan was released from her cage in 1310.

Bruce also freed the veteran warrior, Sir Marmaduke Tweng, without ransom, and sent the bodies of Gloucester and Clifford back to their families, without asking anything in return.

Yet Edward, once home, still flatly refused to recognise Scotland as an independent nation, or indeed Bruce as its king. So the Scots began to make lightning raids into the counties of northern England. There was no end to the War in sight.

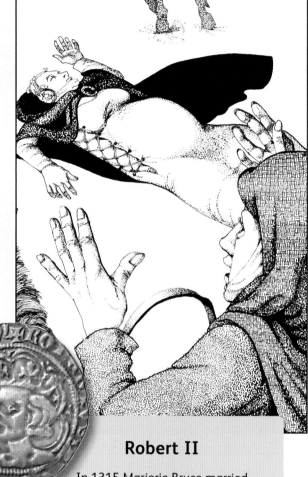

Robert II

In 1315 Marjorie Bruce married the young Walter, 6th hereditary High Steward (Stewart) of Scotland. The following year, while heavily pregnant, she was thrown from her horse and killed. Surgeons delivered the baby, who would eventually become Robert II, the first Stewart King of Scotland.

Bruce was also in trouble with Pope John XXII. In 1309 the previous Pope, Clement V, belatedly excommunicated not only Bruce for killing Comyn in the church, but also those who had helped him in his rise to power.

Pope John refused to recognise Bruce as King of Scotland, addressing letters to him as 'Governor of Scotland'. They were returned unopened. And when Lamberton and three Scottish bishops ignored a summons to attend the papal court in Rome, they too were excommunicated.

Excommunication ...

In 1309 Pope Clement V punished Bruce for the sacrilege of Comyn's murder on church premises. He **excommunicated** him, which meant that he was not allowed to take Communion or to enjoy any other privileges of Church membership.

Bruce still had enemies among those who had supported John Balliol and the Red Comyn. At the parliament held at Scone in August 1320, the 'Black Parliament', twelve people were tried for conspiring against the king. One of them was already dead – his corpse was brought in and set before the judges. Of the rest, three were executed, and two – including the Countess of Strathearn – were sentenced to life imprisonment.

In 1320, eight earls and 31 barons, in the name of the Community of the Realm (the nobles, barons and owners of property), sent a letter to the Pope. It is known as the **Declaration of Arbroath**. Written in beautiful Latin, it is a dignified but firm request to the Pope to persuade Edward II to leave the Scots in peace and to recognise as their King the man of their choice.

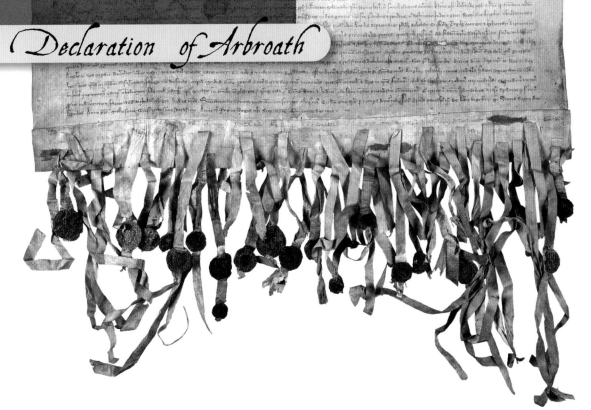

Declaration of Arbroath

Peace at last

David II

In 1324, Bruce's Queen, Elizabeth de Burgh, gave birth to a son, David, who became heir to the throne of Scotland in place of Bruce's grandson, Robert.

The retreat of the English. A truce at last? Renewal of hostilities. How the Scots prove they will never give in.

In 1322 Edward II's army reached Edinburgh and sacked Holyrood Abbey. But Bruce had already ordered all cattle to be sent away from Lothian and food stocks had been destroyed. There was just one lame cow left in the whole region. Finding nothing to eat, the English retreated.

On their way south, the English tried to sack Melrose Abbey, but were scattered by Douglas and his men, lurking in the forest. Bruce now advanced far into England. He broke through the English lines at Scawton Moor with a frontal assault up a steep, rocky hillside. This time he intended to capture Edward II, staying at Rievaulx Abbey.

Edward got away in the nick of time, leaving his personal possessions and silver. After that, the English king agreed to a 13-year truce.

It lasted only four years. In 1327 Edward was forced to abdicate after his queen, Isabella, seized power. He was later murdered. Bruce, unsure whether Isabella's action was lawful and fed up with English pirate attacks on Scottish ships, chose the coronation day of her 14-year-old son, Edward III, to attack Norham Castle in Northumberland.

That summer Douglas and Moray led a Scottish force deep into England. Edward III, with a fine army, marched north to do battle. At first he thought he had caught the Scots at Stanhope Park, but he was to be bitterly disappointed. Instead, after a bold night raid on the English headquarters, the Scottish **hobelars** (mobile cavalry with small, swift horses) vanished into the rain and mist, leaving Edward in tears.

The English retreated to York, and the Scots devastated Northumberland. The English government, realising that the Scots were not going to be beaten, sent envoys to Bruce in Berwick, to ask for peace.

Rievaulx Abbey is an 11th-century former Cistercian abbey near Helmsley, North Yorkshire.

Death of the King

The War comes to an end. A royal wedding. And how the King's remains are buried.

The peace treaty was finally agreed between the two sides in Edinburgh in March 1328 and confirmed by the English parliament in May. The main points were as follows:

* Edward III gave up all claims to rule Scotland and promised to see that the excommunications on Bruce and his subjects were lifted.
* A marriage was arranged between Bruce's heir, David, and Edward's sister, Joan of the Tower.
* The two countries set up a military alliance.
* Bruce paid Edward £20,000, a very large sum for a poor country.

The tomb of Robert the Bruce (below) is at Dunfermline Abbey. Note the carving at the top of the abbey tower.

The royal wedding between David and Joan took place in Berwick in 1328: he was four years old and she just seven. The marriage lasted until her death in 1362, but there were no children.

Though the Pope cancelled the excommunications in 1328, Bruce was now very ill, almost certainly of leprosy. But he insisted on being carried in a litter in slow stages from Girvan to Whithorn. After praying there at the shrine of St Ninian, Bruce was taken back to the royal house he had built at Cardross on the Clyde, where he died on 7 June 1329.

The marriage of David and Joan.

37

His last wish was that his heart should be taken on a crusade to the Holy Land. His body, from which the heart had been cut out, was buried in Dunfermline Abbey. The heart was enclosed in a casket and entrusted to Sir James Douglas. On the way, Douglas went into battle against the Moors in Spain, with the casket hung around his neck on a chain. Douglas died during the battle.

His bones were brought back to Scotland and interred at St Bride's Church, Douglas. The heart of Robert the Bruce is believed now to lie in Melrose Abbey.

Remembering Bruce

Below you will find two rather gruesome mementos of Bruce.

On the left, is a cast of his skull, which plainly shows the ravages of his illness. On the right is a cone-shaped lead container, dating from medieval times, which really does contain an embalmed heart. It was dug up in the chapter house of Melrose Abbey in 1921, and then re-buried. In 1996 it came to light again during an archaeological dig. In June 1998, it was buried once again in the chapter house, under a stone marker.

But is the heart that of Robert the Bruce? No one will ever know for certain as, out of respect for the dead, the container was left unopened.

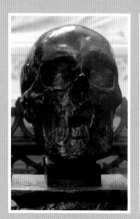

What happened next?

Scotland has two kings.
The unhappy reign of David II.
The defiance of Black Agnes.
How the first Stewart King of Scotland came to the throne.

David II became king at five years old. The War was officially over, but Edward III did not feel bound by the treaty. He supplied troops to John Balliol's son and heir, Edward Balliol, who landed at Kinghorn and marched unopposed to Dupplin, near Scone. Having beaten a much larger Scottish force, he entered Perth in triumph, and had himself crowned at Scone. Scotland now had two kings, and David II was sent to France for safety.

Three famous sons now led the Scottish fightback: John Randolph, son of the Earl of Moray; Marjorie Bruce's son, Robert Stewart, who was now heir to the throne again; and Sir Andrew Murray, the son of Wallace's partner in battle and in government. They were so successful that in 1341 it was felt safe for young David II to return.

By this time Edward III had other things on his mind. In 1339 he had begun the Hundred Years War against France.

David's reign was long and inglorious. In 1346 the King of France asked for help under the treaty (later known as the Auld Alliance) which the Guardians had signed 50 years before. While Edward was occupied in France, David led his army into England, and was defeated and captured at Neville's Cross.

He spent the next eleven years as a closely-guarded prisoner in London.

David returned to Scotland after the first instalment of a large ransom had been paid. By this time Robert Stewart, as Regent of Scotland, had rid the country of the English, and Edward Balliol had given up his crown in return for a comfortable pension. When David died, still childless, in 1371, Robert, now 55, became Robert II, the first Stewart King of Scotland.

A silver penny coin, produced between 1367 and 1371, showing the head of King David II (1324–1371).

Black Agnes

The most celebrated Scottish military engagement of the time was conducted by the Countess of Dunbar, known as 'Black Agnes' because of her dark complexion. While her husband was away with the Scottish army in 1338, she defended Dunbar Castle against a large English force equipped with the latest battering rams and siege catapults. After each barrage, Agnes and her maids, dressed in their best clothes, went around the battlements with dusters, wiping the marks that the huge stones and lead balls had made. At the end of five months, during which she often called down rude remarks at the besiegers, the English gave up and went away.

ANSWERS

Page 9: **Stone of Destiny** – The Stone is currently kept in the Crown Room at Edinburgh Castle alongside the Crown Jewels of Scotland.

Page 21: **Westminster Abbey** – SIR THOMAS MORE and GUY FAWKES.

Page 29: **Detective work** – the defences were destroyed so that should the English regain control they would not be able to defend the castles against the Scots.

What's in a name? – The name 'Wallace' means 'Welshman'.

The Wallace Monument

The National Wallace Monument was built in 1861–69, on Abbey Craig, Stirling. The stained glass window on page 10 features Wallace himself. It is one of four windows in the Hall of Heroes. In total there are 11 stained glass windows, which were installed in the monument in 1885.

FACTS AND ACTIVITIES – ANSWERS

Page ii: **Word search** – Answers below:

F	E	H	T	W	L	L	J	D	R	K	B	Y	U	C	Q	W	W
N	X	X	T	A	O	I	G	A	R	Y	R	P	V	V	D	K	R
D	Q	O	N	I	V	F	G	I	I	V	W	B	G	A	I	V	E
Y	D	A	L	R	X	M	K	S	D	A	J	D	R	N	P	K	D
C	R	L	R	U	A	L	B	L	L	Z	P	P	G	U	Q	C	I
K	A	D	A	N	A	X	P	L	K	R	E	H	V	G	C	R	P
B	S	W	B	F	R	Y	A	M	T	I	O	K	D	U	V	E	S
R	F	S	N	V	B	C	R	N	L	R	R	V	Q	R	W	H	
B	E	B	U	S	E	R	O	I	N	M	T	K	A	H	W	Q	Y
Q	E	D	D	I	S	R	D	N	J	J	Q	H	I	Y	R	Y	I
S	J	D	N	U	W	O	U	G	I	D	P	S	L	Y	O	W	E
O	T	T	W	A	P	O	R	H	T	L	A	C	G	I	N	T	C
S	W	E	Y	A	X	H	X	D	I	A	K	H	C	I	X	T	X
M	U	E	W	G	R	E	T	W	R	C	F	F	C	Y	D	C	Y
D	S	M	P	A	N	D	L	G	R	A	V	U	W	D	O	T	Q
E	R	W	I	G	R	E	P	A	Z	O	C	C	Q	Q	T	J	F
T	C	O	Q	R	R	D	W	S	H	E	S	E	L	R	I	G	F
D	N	A	L	E	R	I	D	T	O	A	B	P	B	Z	B	E	D

Page iv–v: **Criss crossword** – Answers below:

		W	I	L	L	I	A	M		C	A	L	T	H	R	O	P
		S		O			A									E	
A	D	A		N			I					P				R	
R		B		D			D	A	V	I	D		O			T	
M		E		O		D		Y			U		P			H	
Y	O	L	A	N	D	E	R			N		E					
		L				F				B							
		A	B	B	E	Y			G	U	A	R	D	I	A	N	S
		O					H			R							I
		F			C		O					W					X
O		M	A	L	C	O	L	M		E	L	E	A	N	O	R	
C		A			M		A					L					C
H	A	R	R	Y			Y		G			L					R
I			E		N		E		E	D	W	A	R	D			U
L			L						C								S
S	T	I	R	L	I	N	G				T	W	E	N	G		A
			E														D
		D	E	V	O	R	G	U	I	L	L	A					E

Page vi: **Who am I?** – (A) King Robert I ('The Bruce'); (B) Princess Margaret, the Maid of Norway; (C) King Edward I of England; (D) King Alexander III; (E) King David II; (F) King Edward II of England; (G) King Robert II; (H) King John (Balliol, 'Toom Tabard').

Wallace and Bruce

Facts and activities

A! Fredome is a noble thing
Fredom mays man to haiff liking
Fredom all solace to man giffis
He levys at es that frely levys ...

From *The Bruce*
by John Barbour (*c*.1320–95)

mays = makes
liking = pleasure
solace = comfort
levys = lives

Word search

There are 18 words below related to Robert the Bruce and William Wallace. They are hidden in this word square. Can you find them?

Answers on page 40

F	E	H	T	W	L	L	J	D	R	K	B	Y	U	C	Q	W	W
N	X	X	T	A	O	I	G	A	R	Y	R	P	V	V	D	K	R
D	Q	O	N	I	V	F	G	I	I	V	W	B	G	A	I	V	E
Y	D	A	L	R	X	M	K	S	D	A	J	D	R	N	P	K	D
C	R	L	R	U	A	L	B	L	L	Z	P	P	G	U	Q	C	I
K	A	D	A	N	A	X	P	L	K	R	E	H	V	G	C	R	P
B	S	W	B	F	R	Y	A	M	T	I	O	K	D	U	V	E	S
R	F	S	N	V	B	C	R	N	L	R	R	R	V	Q	R	W	H
B	E	B	U	S	E	R	O	I	N	M	T	K	A	H	W	Q	Y
Q	E	D	D	I	S	R	D	N	J	J	Q	H	I	Y	R	Y	I
S	J	D	N	U	W	O	U	G	I	D	P	S	L	Y	O	W	E
O	T	T	W	A	P	O	R	H	T	L	A	C	G	I	N	T	C
S	W	E	Y	A	X	H	X	D	I	A	K	H	C	I	X	T	X
M	U	E	W	G	R	E	T	W	R	C	F	F	C	Y	D	C	Y
D	S	M	P	A	N	D	L	G	R	A	V	U	W	D	O	T	Q
E	R	W	I	G	R	E	P	A	Z	O	C	C	Q	Q	T	J	F
T	C	O	Q	R	R	D	W	S	H	E	S	E	L	R	I	G	F
D	N	A	L	E	R	I	D	T	O	A	B	P	B	Z	B	E	D

ALEXANDER	EDWARD	NORWAY	You can move
BALLIOL	FALKIRK	RAGMAN	diagonally, as well
BRUCE	HESELRIG	SPIDER	as up and down, in
CALTHROP	IRELAND	STEWARD	any direction, to
CARDROSS	KINGHORN	TWENG	find the words
DUNBAR	LANARK	WALLACE	listed.

Make a game of Bannockburn chequers

You will need:

- ❏ a piece of card 15 x 15 cm square
- ❏ card to make figures
- ❏ soft modelling clay for bases

Rule the board into 3 cm squares. Colour them alternately black and white. Make five Scottish and five English warriors out of the card. You can see how to dress them from illustrations in this book. Stick them into bases of soft modelling clay.

The rules are the same as draughts. First player to capture all the enemy wins!

Despite being shown in films such as *Braveheart* wearing kilts and tartans, Scottish warriors were more likely to have worn saffron-coloured tunics called *leine croich*, a knee-length shirt of leather, linen or canvas, heavily pleated and sometimes quilted as protection. The linen tunics were dyed with horse urine or bark to create the yellow colour. Armour and weapons of a knight of the time would include a great helmet, a sword, mail sleeves, leg-coverings, and a shield as shown (right) on the seal of Robert II and in the battle depiction (near right).

Criss crossword

See page v opposite. Clues across are marked with numbers.
Clues down are marked with letters.

Answers on page 40

Across

1. King of Scotland 1165–1214.
2. Device for laming the enemy's horses.
3. Wife of Count Holland.
4. Son of Robert I.
5. French wife of Alexander III.
6. Residence of monks.
7. Rulers of Scotland after death of King Alexander III.
8. King of Scotland 1153–65.
9. Mother of John Comyn.
10. Blind _____.
11. 'The Hammer of the Scots'.
12. Battle of _____ Bridge.
13. Brave enemy spared by Wallace.
14. Founder of Sweetheart Abbey (below), Lady _____.

Down

A. First wife of Robert the Bruce.
B. Birthplace of King Edward I.
C. The _____ of Norway.
D. City near Scone.
E. Body of soldiers.
F. He excommunicated Robert the Bruce.
G. Earl of Gloucester retreated to _____ in 1307.
H. Where Black Agnes dusted the battlements _____ Castle.
I. To refuse to obey.
J. The original number of Guardians of Scotland in 1286.
K. In 1292 John Balliol swore _____ to King Edward I.
L. Surname of man murdered by Bruce at Dumfries.
M. Executed in London in 1305.
N. Abbey Craig is an outcrop of these hills.
O. Douglas took the heart of Bruce on _____.
P. A war-cry was this.
Q. Colour and nickname of John Comyn.

Sweetheart Abbey

Make a calthrop

A real calthrop was made of two pieces of iron twisted and welded together. You can make a model with two lengths of bendable wire (garden wire is good) about 20 cm long, or two craft pipe-cleaners. When you drop the calthrop on the floor, three of the spikes must form a tripod for the fourth. If it doesn't, work on your design!

Who am I?

Test your knowledge of Kings and Queens!
The following individuals are mentioned by name in this book.
Can you work out who they are from the clues?
Write the name of the person on the last line.

Answers on page 40

Person A:

Born:	1274
at:	Turnberry, Ayrshire
parents:	Robert Bruce, Lord of Annandale, and Marjorie, Countess of Carrick
married:	1. Isabel of Mar 2. Elizabeth de Burgh
lived in:	Scotland, Ireland
crowned:	1306 at Scone
died:	1329
at:	Cardross, near Dumbarton
of:	leprosy

I am _____

Person B:

Born:	c.1283
at:	Tønsberg, Norway
parents:	King Eric II of Norway and Margaret of Scotland
married:	No one
lived in:	Norway
crowned:	never
died:	1290
at:	South Ronaldsay, Orkney
of:	(probably) sea-sickness

I am _____

Person C:

Born:	1239
at:	London
parents:	King Henry III of England and Eleanor of Provence
married:	Eleanor of Castille
lived in:	England, France
crowned:	1274 at Westminster
died:	1307
at:	Burgh-on-Sands
of:	natural causes

I am _____

Person D:

Born:	1241
at:	Roxburgh
parents:	King Alexander II of Scotland and Marie de Coucy
married:	1. Margaret of England 2. Yolande de Dreux
lived in:	Scotland
crowned:	1249 at Scone
died:	1285
at:	Kinghorn
of:	a riding accident

I am _____

Person E:

Born:	1324
at:	Dunfermline
parents:	King Robert I of Scotland and Elizabeth de Burgh
married:	Joan of England
lived in:	Scotland, France, England
crowned:	1329 at Scone
died:	1371
at:	Edinburgh
of:	natural causes

I am _____

Person F:

Born:	1284
at:	Caernarvon, Wales
parents:	King Edward I of England and Eleanor of Provence
married:	Isabella of France
lived in:	Wales, England, France
crowned:	1307 at Westminster
died:	1327
at:	Berkeley Castle, Gloucestershire
of:	murdered

I am _____

Person G:

Born:	1316
at:	Paisley
parents:	Walter the Steward and Marjorie Bruce
married:	1. Elizabeth Mure
	2. Euphemia of Moray
lived in:	Scotland
crowned:	1371 at Scone
died:	1390
at:	Dundonald Castle, Ayrshire
of:	natural causes

I am _____

Person H:

Born:	1249
at:	(probably) Barnard Castle, Co. Durham
parents:	John Barnard of Barnard Castle and Devorguilla of Galloway
married:	Isabel de Warenne
lived in:	Scotland, England, France
crowned:	1295 at Scone
died:	1315
at:	Bailleul, Normandy
of:	natural causes

I am _____

Dunfermline Palace

PLACES OF INTEREST

Places to visit with connections to William Wallace or Robert the Bruce. As opening times may vary, check details with the local Tourist Information Office.

National Wallace Monument
Causewayhead, Stirling
www.nationalwallacemonument.com

Bannockburn Visitor Centre
www.nts.org.uk

Arbroath Abbey
www.historic-scotland.gov.uk

Heart of Bruce Burial Site, Melrose Abbey
www.historic-scotland.gov.uk

National Museums Scotland
www.nms.ac.uk

Edinburgh Castle
www.edinburghcastle.gov.uk

Robert the Bruce Trail
Dumfries and Galloway, takes you back 700 years, covering where Bruce grew up.

Stirling Castle
www.stirlingcastle.gov.uk

Sweetheart Abbey
www.historicscotland.gov.uk

Scone Palace
www.scone-palace.co.uk

FURTHER CREDITS

SCOTTISH PICTURES, DRAWN WITH PEN AND PENCIL by Samuel Gosnell Green (Religious Tract Society: London, 1891) – for pp 8 (Dunbar Castle); 19 (Bothwell Castle): Facts and activities section – i (Wallace Monument); vii (Dunfermline Palace)

THE COMPREHENSIVE HISTORY OF ENGLAND: Civil, Military, Religious, Intellectual and Social – Macfarlane and Thomson (Blackie & Son: Glasgow, n.d.) – for pages 9 (Edward I's tomb); 14 (Battle of Stirling Bridge); 21 (Wallace's execution); 31 (Battle of Bannockburn)

© BOB COWAN – for pages 5 (Alexander III memorial); 23 (Greyfriars Kirk, Dumfries, plaque and Sweetheart Abbey); 27 (Lanercost Priory); 37 (Dunfermline Abbey and tomb of Robert the Bruce); 38 (skull and Melrose Abbey): Facts and activities section – v (Sweetheart Abbey)

ANTONY KAMM – for pages 2–3 (genealogical chart)

© NASA – for page 13 (map of Scotland)

© NATIONAL LIBRARY OF SCOTLAND – for pages 11 (Blind Harry extract, Adv.Ms.19.2.2 [ii] f55 verso); 24 (Seton Armorial, NLS Acc.9309.f.9)

NATIONAL RECORDS OF SCOTLAND – (© Crown Copyright, National Records of Scotland)
– for page 28 (SP13/3, Letter by the Magnates of Scotland to King Philip IV of France regarding the right of King Robert I to the Crown of Scotland, 16 March 1309)
– for page 35 (SP13/7, Declaration of Arbroath, 6 April 1320)

© THE NATIONAL WALLACE MONUMENT – page 40 (Monument)

© LYNNE REILLY – for page 36 (Rievaulx Abbey)

THE ROMAN WALL – Rev. J Collingwood Bruce (Longman, Green, Reader and Dyer, Newcastle-upon-Tyne, 1807) – Facts and activities section page v (calthrops)

ROYAL COLLECTION – (Royal Collection Trust / © Her Majesty Queen Elizabeth II 2014) – for pp 7 (Edward I); 32 (Edward II)

ROYAL COMMISSION ON THE ANCIENT & HISTORICAL MONUMENTS OF SCOTLAND – (© RCAHMS [Aerial Photography Collection] Licensor www.rcahms.gov.uk) – for page 15 (Stirling)

SCRAN
– for page 7 (John Balliol, from Foreman Memorial) (© National Library of Scotland / Licensor www.scran.ac.uk)
– for page 10 (stained-glass window) (© Stirling District Tourism Ltd / Licensor www.scran.ac.uk)
– for page 12 (Dunnottar Castle) (© Crown Copyright reproduced courtesy of Historic Scotland / Licensor www.scran.ac.uk)
– for page 22 (Turnberry Castle) (© South Ayrshire Libraries Local History Collection, Ayr Carnegie Library / Licensor www.scran.ac.uk)
– for page 27 (Louden Hill) (© West of Scotland Archaeology Service / Licensor www.scran.ac.uk)
– for page 33 (statue of Robert I) (© National Trust for Scotland / Licensor www.scran.ac.uk)
– for page 38 (lead container) (© Crown Copyright reproduced courtesy of Historic Scotland / Licensor www.scran.ac.uk)

© JOHN DOUGLAS WILSON – for page 16 (Stirling Castle)

OTHER TITLES IN THE SCOTTIES SERIES
(eds Frances and Gordon Jarvie)

The Clans (Gordon Jarvie)

The Covenanters (Claire Watts)

Flight in Scotland (Frances and Gordon Jarvie)

Greyfriars Bobby: A Tale of Victorian Edinburgh (Frances and Gordon Jarvie)

The Jacobites (Antony Kamm)

Mary, Queen of Scots (Elizabeth Douglas)

Robert Burns in Time and Place (Frances and Gordon Jarvie)

The Romans in Scotland (Frances Jarvie)

Scotland's Vikings (Frances and Gordon Jarvie)

Scottish Explorers (Antony Kamm)

Scottish Kings and Queens (Elizabeth Douglas)

Scottish Rocks and Fossils (Alan and Moira McKirdy)

Supernatural Scotland (Eileen Dunlop)

There shall be a Scottish Parliament (Frances and Gordon Jarvie)